Scientific Advancements of the 19th Century

Auguste & Louis Lumière

and the Rise of Motion Pictures

Mitchell Lane
PUBLISHERS

P.O. Box 196
Hockessin, Delaware 19707

Uncharted, Unexplored, and Unexplained

Scientific Advancements of the 19th Century

Titles in the Series

Visit us on the web: www.mitchelllane.com
Comments? email us: mitchelllane@mitchelllane.com

Uncharted, Unexplored, and Unexplained

Scientific Advancements of the 19th Century

Auguste & Louis Lumière

and the Rise of Motion Pictures

Jim Whiting

Uncharted, Unexplored, and Unexplained

Scientific Advancements of the 19th Century

Copyright © 2006 by Mitchell Lane Publishers, Inc. All rights reserved. No part of this book may be reproduced without written permission from the publisher. Printed and bound in the United States of America.

Printing   1   2   3   4   5   6   7   8   9

Library of Congress Cataloging-in-Publication Data
Whiting, Jim, 1943–
    Auguste and Louis Lumière and the rise of motion pictures / by Jim Whiting.
        p. cm. — (Uncharted, unexplored, and unexplained)
    Includes bibliographical references and index.
    ISBN 1-58415-365-2 (library bound)
    1. Cinematography—History. 2. Motion pictures—History. I. Title. II. Series.
TR848.W45 2005
778.5'3'09—dc22

                                                                    2005009703

ABOUT THE AUTHOR: Jim Whiting has been a remarkably versatile and accomplished journalist, writer, editor and photographer for more than 30 years. A voracious reader since early childhood, Mr. Whiting has written and edited about 200 nonfiction children's books. His subjects range from authors to zoologists and include contemporary pop icons and classical musicians, saints and scientists, emperors and explorers. Representative titles include *The Life and Times of Franz Liszt, The Life and Times of Julius Caesar, Charles Schulz, Charles Darwin and the Origin of the Species,* and *Juan Ponce de Leon.*

    Other career highlights are a lengthy stint publishing *Northwest Runner,* the first piece of original fiction to appear in *Runners World* magazine, hundreds of descriptions and venue photographs for America Online, e-commerce product writing, sports editor for the *Bainbridge Island Review,* light verse in a number of magazines, and acting as the official photographer for the Antarctica Marathon.

    He lives in Washington State with his wife and two teenage sons.

PHOTO CREDITS: Cover, pp. 1, 3, 36—Time Life Pictures/Mansell/Getty Images; pp. 9, 12 top, 14—Library of Congress; pp. 10, 20—Victorian Cinema; pp. 12 bottom, 22, 30—Hulton Archive/Getty Images; pp. 19, 33—Smithsonian Institution; pp. 40, 41 top—Audio Heritage; p. 41 bottom—Lumière Institute.

PUBLISHER'S NOTE: This story is based on the author's extensive research, which he believes to be accurate. Documentation of such research is on page 46.

The internet sites referenced herein were active as of the publication date. Due to the fleeting nature of some websites, we cannot guarantee they will all be active when you are reading this book.

Uncharted, Unexplored, and Unexplained

Scientific Advancements of the 19th Century

Auguste & Louis Lumière

and the Rise of Motion Pictures

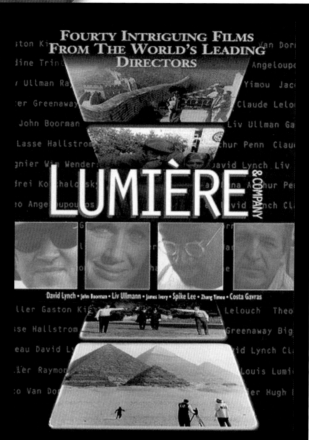

This is the cover of the video recording of *Lumière and Company*. The recording consists of one-minute movies produced in 1995 by forty prominent filmmakers. They all used the same camera that Louis Lumière invented in 1895. The camera still worked perfectly.

1

Billion Dollar Baby

In 1995, movie audiences flocked to see *Toy Story*, the first completely computer-animated feature film. It was the initial production of Pixar Animation Studios. Pixar would subsequently release *A Bug's Life*; *Monsters, Inc.*; *Finding Nemo*; and *The Incredibles*.

Another audience favorite that year was *Jumanji*. Star Robin Williams and two children are trapped inside a frightening board game. One of the most memorable scenes shows a herd of wild animals stampeding through the streets of town. The stampede is a computer-generated special effect.

The winner of the Academy Award for Best Picture in 1995 was *Braveheart*. Mel Gibson was the producer, the director, and the star of the film. It told the story of the struggle of Scotland against England at the end of the 13th century. Like *Toy Story* and *Jumanji*, the film employed state-of-the-art equipment. Computer animation was used to show some very realistic and gruesome battle scenes.

That same year, 40 of the world's most famous movie directors collaborated on another screen project. The project was a film entitled *Lumière and Company*. The film honored the 100th anniversary of the first commercial movie exhibition. The group of directors also used state-of-the-art equipment—from 1895.

Of course that equipment was a far cry from the technical marvels of a century later. The camera was contained in a small wooden box. It weighed just 16 pounds. It was operated by a hand crank. It could take only about 50 seconds of film. It had no capability for recording sound.

This camera had been invented in France by two brothers, Louis and Auguste Lumière. Their craftsmanship was so good that the 40 directors were able to use the very same camera that the brothers had designed. It still worked perfectly. The directors set out to imitate what the Lumières had accomplished. They had to work under the same conditions. They had to keep the camera in one position. They couldn't record any sound. Like the originals, their films could only be about 50 seconds long. And they could only do three takes.

Each director was asked why he or she would want to undertake such a project. It certainly wasn't for the money. Some said they wanted to show their appreciation for the Lumières' invention. Others explained that to make a film using such primitive equipment would be a welcome challenge. A few added that it would be a thrill to operate the original camera.

The Lumières are credited with the first public film showing. But they didn't invent motion pictures, or movies, as they soon came to be known. Almost from the time that their countryman, Joseph Nicéphore Niepce, made what is considered to be the world's first photograph in 1826, there was a desire to give motion to these pictures.

The first major breakthrough came about half a century after the first photo. In 1872, California Governor Leland Stanford hired photographer Eadweard Muybridge to settle a $25,000 bet with a friend. Stanford owned a string of racehorses. He was sure that at some point all four hooves of a galloping horse were off the ground. His friend said otherwise. After five years of experimentation, Muybridge set up a row of 24 cameras along a racetrack. The shutter of each camera was attached to a string that stretched across the track. As the horse hurtled along the track, it tripped the shutters in rapid succession. When the photos were developed, they proved that Stanford was right. He was delighted, even though Muybridge's work had cost him $40,000. He didn't mind that he'd lost $15,000 to win his bet. He was one of the wealthiest men in the country.

Muybridge spent 20 more years perfecting this multi-camera technique. To exhibit his work, he invented a device called the zoopraxiscope. It was just one of a number of similar inventions with tongue-twisting names that sprang up during the 19th century as inventors tried to create the illusion of motion: Actograph. Andersonoscopograph. Biograph. Choreutoscope. Eknetograph. Electrotachyscope. Phototachygraph. Scenematograph. And many more.

There was also the Chronophotograph. It was the brainchild of the Frenchman Étienne-Jules Marey.

Eadweard Muybridge was born in England in 1830. He moved to the United States as an adult. He did pioneering photographic work showing the motion of humans and animals. He took hundreds of thousands of photographs before his death in 1904.

Resembling a shotgun, its "barrel" was actually a long lens. Behind the lens was a circular chamber that held a photographic plate. The plate rotated in a full circle in a single second, making 12 exposures. Eventually his device could contain 150 separate images. Even though Marey's primary interest was analyzing movement rather than creating it, he went one step beyond Muybridge. He recorded his images on a long strip of photographic paper that would pass in front of a lens. But he couldn't figure out a way to provide the strip with regular motion.

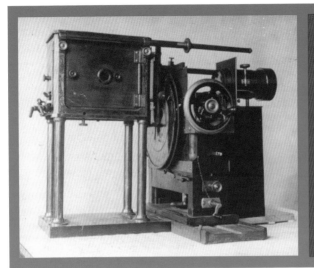

One of Muybridge's most notable achievements was the zoopraxiscope. It showed individual images in rapid succession. He used it during lectures in the United States and England.

There was no exotic name for the device constructed around 1887 by yet another Frenchman, Louis Aimé Augustin Le Prince. It was very similar to what the Lumière brothers would invent several years later. But Le Prince vanished in 1890. So did his invention.

By then, the famous American inventor Thomas Edison had met both Muybridge and Marey. His restless, creative mind latched on to motion pictures. Edison had invented the phonograph in 1877. He said he wanted something that would do for people's eyes what the phonograph did for their ears. In conjunction with William Dickson, one of his best employees, Edison at first tried to adapt the cylinder mechanism he made for the phonograph. When that mechanism didn't

This strip helped Leland Stanford win his bet. The image in the lower left shows a horse with all four hooves in the air.

work, he and Dickson devised a roller with toothed sprockets. These sprockets corresponded with perforations in each side of the film. That way the film would pass by the lens at a uniform speed.

Called the Kinetograph, their invention took advantage of George Eastman's new celluloid photographic material. Eastman was the founder of the Eastman Kodak Company. He coated celluloid with a light-sensitive emulsion and manufactured it in long strips. Edison and Dickson used this film for what most film historians regard as the first moving pictures. To show these films, Dickson invented the Kinetoscope. The device was a large cabinet with a peephole. Customers would insert a coin, then lean over the peephole and view films inside the cabinet.

Two important figures in movie development: George Eastman (left) invented movie film. Thomas Edison (right) made cameras and projectors.

Edison and Dickson knew that they would need to provide a great deal of material for the Kinetoscope parlors. The Kinetograph was a massive device. It weighed well over half a ton and ran using electrical current. It was far too bulky to be taken from place to place. Dickson built a studio called the Black Maria to contain the Kinetograph. It also gave him a convenient site for his filming. It was an odd-looking shed, measuring about 20 feet by 30 feet. Part of the roof would open to

admit sunlight, the only reliable source of lighting. The Black Maria was mounted on a turntable. It slowly turned and followed the sun's path across the sky.

Dickson had a steady stream of performers. They ranged from vaudeville and circus acts to boxers and actors. They all were eager to promote their theatrical productions. There was also a steady stream of paying customers when the first Kinetoscope parlors opened in New York. The craze soon spread to other American cities and major foreign capitals.

One of those foreign capitals was Paris, France. The Kinetoscope was as popular there as it had been elsewhere. One of the thousands of patrons who packed the Kinetoscope parlors was especially interested in the technical aspects of the presentation. He was a photographer named Antoine Lumière. To nearly everyone else, Edison's accomplishment offered entertainment. To Lumière, it offered opportunity.

Movie Mystery

While mysteries would eventually become one of the most popular film forms, the historical development of motion pictures includes a real-life mystery. It involves Louis Aimé Augustin Le Prince, a Frenchman who is virtually forgotten today.

Born in 1842, he became involved in photography at a young age. Louis Daguerre, who invented the first practical means of making photographic portraits, was a family friend. He took an interest in Louis and showed the boy some of his techniques. Le Prince moved to Leeds, England, when he was a young man and married soon afterward. With his wife, he opened an art school. He developed a way of putting colored photos on metal and ceramics. He also became well known as a photographer, even doing work for Queen Victoria.

Louis Daguerre, above, taught Louis Le Prince about photography.

He probably became interested in making motion pictures after viewing some of Eadweard Muybridge's work. This interest continued when he and his family moved to New York City in 1881. His wife taught at a school for the deaf. Le Prince obtained permission to use the school's workshop and tools for his photographic work. One day his daughter opened the door to the workshop. She saw moving pictures on the wall.

The family returned to England in 1887. Le Prince applied for a patent for a camera that was capable of taking motion pictures. He began using his camera to photograph scenes in Leeds. In 1889, he built a projector that would show the images on a screen. He now had all the elements for motion picture photography and projection that would eventually become standard.

In August 1890, Le Prince crossed the English Channel to France on business. Then he went to the city of Dijon to visit his brother. On September 16, he boarded a train that would take him to Paris. He never arrived. Both he and his baggage completely vanished. Detectives made an investigation. They couldn't find any clues to his mysterious disappearance. No one ever discovered what happened to him.

Antoine Lumière became interested in photography as a young man. After early struggles, the company he ran with his two sons became very successful. In later life he used some of his fortune to purchase several expensive homes. He died in 1911.

2

The Cinématographe

Antoine Lumière was born in eastern France in 1840. Married at the age of 19, he settled in the city of Besançon. He began his working life as a sign painter. Soon he moved on to painting portraits. He became caught up in the relatively new invention of photography. He established a photographic studio that specialized in portraits. With his name, it was a fitting career move. *Lumière* means "light." The basic principle of photography is admitting a controlled amount of light onto film. In 1870 the threat of a German invasion prompted him to move his family to Lyon, France's second most important commercial center. He eventually moved beyond portraiture to set up a thriving business manufacturing photographic supplies.

By then he had two sons, Auguste (born on October 19, 1862) and Louis (born on October 5, 1864). The boys attended La Martinière, the largest technical school in Lyon. They went to work in the family firm when they were in their mid-teens. It didn't take long for Louis to make an impact. In 1881, when he was just 17, he developed a high-quality photographic plate. The plates were an instant success. They became the primary source of profit for the company. At its peak, the firm produced upward of 15 million plates per year. It was the second largest photographic company in the world, behind Eastman Kodak.

According to most accounts, Antoine was the "idea man" in the business. Seeing the Kinetoscope gave him one of his best ideas. As one of the firm's employees, Eugène Molsson, recalled, "It was in Summer 1894. Papa [Antoine] Lumière entered my office where I was with Louis and took out of his pocket a bit of a Kinetoscope film that he had gotten from Edison's agents and said to Louis: 'This is what you should make, because Edison sells it at insane prices and his representatives are looking to make them here in France to have a better deal.' "[1]

To make pictures—moving or otherwise—required a camera. Despite Antoine's words to Louis, Auguste was the brother who made the first attempts to build one. When he couldn't succeed, Louis took over the task. At first, he, too, had little success.

For much of his life, Louis often suffered from headaches and insomnia. It was late in 1894, on one of the nights when he couldn't sleep, that he solved the basic problem.

A still camera operates on a simple principle. A shutter opens for a short period of time. The opening admits light through the lens onto the film behind the lens. The light creates an image of whatever is within range of the lens. Then the shutter closes to prevent further light—which would overexpose the image—from reaching the film.

A movie camera employs the same principle. The difference is that the shutter has to keep opening and closing to create a succession of individual images. When an image has been exposed, the film has to be advanced. The next time the shutter opens, it will make a new image on an unexposed piece of film.

On that sleepless night, Louis envisioned how that film advance could take place. He thought of a sewing machine. A sewing machine holds fabric motionless while the needle and thread make a stitch. The machine quickly advances the fabric between stitches. Then it holds the fabric motionless for the next stitch. Louis applied the same principle to his camera. When the shutter closed each time, a set of claws would engage perforations on each side of the film. The claws would pull the film along. Then they would release. That would leave the film steady while the shutter opened. When the shutter closed again, the claws would move the film to the next frame. The frames would be separated by a black band (the result of the film not receiving any light). When the film was played back, the frames would appear in rapid succession. The human eye couldn't distinguish each individual image. Rather, it would perceive the slight differences between frames as motion. This stop-and-go sequence is known as intermittent movement. It remains one of the basic principles of motion picture photography.

Louis's background in photography took him in an entirely different direction from Edison and Dickson. Their camera—the Kinetograph—was massive. Louis was used to the handheld cameras for which his firm supplied film. He "thought small to think big." His camera, even with the added weight of a hand crank to advance the film, weighed just 16 pounds.

He added two more elements to his invention. One element made the camera capable of printing film from the negatives it created. The other, far more important for the development of the film industry, allowed projection. Auguste noted, "We had observed, my brother and I, how interesting it would be if we could project on a screen, and show before a whole gathering, animated scenes faithfully reproducing objects and people in movement."[2]

Projection also involved intermittent motion. As each frame of film passed in front of the projector lens, it was held motionless for a moment while the shutter opened. Then the shutter would close and the film would advance to the next frame. At this point the shutter would open again. As with filming, this continual opening and shutting occurred 16 times per second. The beam of light constantly going on and off made the film appear to flicker. This phenomenon gave movies yet another nickname: "flickers," or the more common "flicks." While movie projectors operate in much the same fashion today, advances in technology have virtually eliminated the flickering. But the nickname persists.

For the first time, it would become possible to show motion pictures to an audience. Edison's Kinetoscope was limited to a single viewer at a time.

The Lumières felt a great deal of urgency. They knew other people were working on similar ideas. Their new device had to work reliably. It also had to be introduced as quickly as possible. The Lumières had one big advantage over their potential rivals: their company. It had the prestige of an established business. It earned a lot of money. The money gave them financial resources to dedicate to their invention. Lone wolf inventors such as the unfortunate Le Prince faced an uphill battle in developing and marketing their devices.

Louis called his invention the Cinématographe. The word literally means "written movement." With its lightweight, simple operating mechanism, and its ability to perform three functions, the Cinématographe was a technological marvel.

The Cinématographe itself has long since been superseded by more advanced equipment. But the name survives in several related words. Shortened to *cinema,* it is the preferred term for movies in many countries. *Cinematography* is the term used for the art of movie photography. *Cinematographers* are the people who do the actual filming.

Their camera wasn't the only legacy the Lumières left to the film industry. The width of their film was the now-standard 35 millimeters, or just less than an inch and a half. Their rate of exposure of 16 frames per second became standard. That allowed them to shoot about 50 seconds of film. By contrast, Edison's equipment worked at the rate of 46 frames per second, and his films were only about 16 seconds long. (The film they worked with was so brittle that longer pieces would break.)

In contrast to Edison's cumbersome equipment, the Cinématographe was portable. Its operators could go almost anywhere and film almost anything. It also allowed for a quick turnaround time. It became possible to shoot film in the morning, process it in the afternoon, and show it to an audience in the evening.

The brothers patented their invention on February 13, 1895, and made their first film on March 19, 1895. They set up their equipment near the entrance to the family factory and filmed the well-dressed workers as they left the premises. The film, which also includes a passing horse and a dog that bounds in and out of the scene, is called *Workers Leaving the Lumière Factory.* The street onto which the workers exited was known at the time as the Chemin Saint Victor. It has since been renamed Rue du Premier Film (Street of the First Film).

The brothers took their Cinématographe and their film to Paris. They displayed them to the Society for the Encouragement of National Industry. The brothers conducted a series of private showings. These showings were designed to gain advance publicity and to position their invention in advance of the numerous competitors. They were successful in both endeavors.

One of their most important demonstrations came in June back in

This device revolutionized motion pictures. Called the Cinématographe, it was patented by Louis and Auguste Lumière early in 1895. Its small size and light weight made it ideal for shooting in a variety of settings.

Lyon, to the Congress of the French Photographic Society. The brothers filmed members of the group getting off an excursion boat. They also filmed a conversation between the noted astronomer Pierre-Jules-César Janssen and a man named Lagrange. They screened the films the following evening. The society's members were doubly impressed—by

A drawing of Louis Lumière making one of his films. At first he was the company's primary photographer. As the company expanded its movie business, he oversaw camera production and the training of cameramen.

the technical accomplishment and by the fact that they had been included in the demonstration. The workers leaving the Lumière factory were anonymous. None of them established eye contact with the camera. The Society members wanted to make sure that they were recognized. Nearly all tipped their hat or waved to the cameraman. They returned home with great praise for what they had seen.

When they weren't on the road, the brothers continued shooting to provide more films for their demonstrations. Louis was by far the more productive brother. It is likely that Auguste made only a single film.

The brothers originally made the films to demonstrate what their camera could do. They probably thought it would appeal to the same people who bought equipment and supplies for still photography. Now they realized the primary market for their invention wasn't selling individual Cinématographes. Profits would come from holding public exhibitions—and charging admission.

It was time to put the theory to the test.

Thomas Edison using his phonograph

Thomas Edison was born on February 11, 1847, in Milan, Ohio. When he began school, he was very hyperactive. His teacher kicked him out of class. His mother had to homeschool him. A voracious reader, he devoured many of the books in the local library.

At the age of 12, he began publishing a newspaper. He sold copies to train passengers. A few years later, he became a telegraph operator. In 1868, he moved to Boston, Massachusetts, to work for the Western Union Company. In his spare time, his natural curiosity led him to work on his own projects. His first invention was an electric vote-counting machine. No one was interested. The experience taught him a valuable lesson: He would only work on things that would sell.

With almost no money in his pocket, he moved to New York. By a stroke of luck, he happened to be in the office of a stockbroker when a stock ticker broke down. The man was panic-stricken. Edison took a quick glance at the machine and fixed it. The man offered him a job. With a steady income, Edison could afford to resume his experimental work. He invented an improved stock ticker. He sold it for $40,000, a huge sum in that era. That money and the money from other inventions gave him enough to open his own laboratory.

In 1877, Edison invented the phonograph. He also made an improved version of the telephone. In 1879, he invented the first practical incandescent lightbulb. Several years later, he devised a way to generate and distribute electrical power throughout an entire city. Many consider that to be his greatest achievement.

In 1887, he opened the world's first research and development center in West Orange, New Jersey. In addition to the Kinetoscope and Kinetograph, the center also produced such devices as the dictaphone, mimeograph, and storage battery. In World War I, Edison helped the U.S. government solve technical problems.

In all, he was awarded more than 1,000 patents. Shortly after his death on October 18, 1931, businesses and homes all over the world briefly turned off their electric power to honor him.

A still image from the first Lumière film, *Workers Leaving the Lumière Factory*. The film begins with the factory doors shut. Moments later, they open. Scores of workers spill into the street. The film ends when the last one has left the building.

3

Filming Around the World

Temperamentally, Antoine Lumière was the family member best suited for organizing a public exhibition. As France's largest city, Paris was the logical site.

Antoine rented a basement room in the Grand Café. It was a restaurant on one of the city's busiest streets. A man stood outside, announcing to passersby what was about to take place. Most people ignored him. The relative handful who responded—35 in all, each of whom paid one franc admission—went down a flight of stairs. As they entered the room, they received printed programs listing the 10 films to be shown. A white sheet covered part of one wall. The Cinématographe sat on a stool near the opposite wall. Antoine hired a piano player. The music would provide an alternative sound to the somewhat noisy projector. It would also entertain the patrons while the operator changed the films.

The main lights were turned off and the light just behind the projector was turned on. At first the image on the screen was unmoving. The audience must have been a bit disappointed. Then the operator began cranking the Cinématographe. Suddenly the static image began to move. Workers poured out of a factory, turned left or right, and disappeared from the frame. They were replaced by other workers in a display of constant motion. Nine other films followed *Workers Leaving the Lumière Factory*: *Horseback Jumping, Fishing for Goldfish, Landing of Photographic Congress Members at Lyon, The Blacksmiths, A Little Trick on the Gardener, Feeding the Baby, Blanket Toss, The Place des Cordeliers in Lyon,* and *The Sea.*

It was December 28, 1895—the day the motion picture industry was born.

While the Lumières may have been disturbed by the meager turnout, they didn't need to worry. Word quickly spread. Within three weeks, the demand to see the films was so great that they were doing multiple shows every day. Their daily grosses exceeded 2,000 francs. People waited patiently in long lines. Sometimes they grew impatient and fistfights broke out. Policemen had to be called in to restore order.

Every few weeks the program would change. Probably each one began with *Workers Leaving the Lumière Factory*. It was their signature piece. The film conveyed a not-so-subtle message. Dozens of workers pour through the gate. They all are very well dressed. They couldn't wear such fine clothing if they weren't earning good money. The company paid them high wages because it was very large and very successful.

Another commercial message occurs in *The Card Game*. Antoine Lumière faces another man and begins dealing cards. Seated between them, facing the camera, is the brothers' father-in-law (Auguste and Louis married sisters). He owned a local brewery. While the other two men are concentrating on their game, the father-in-law signals for a waiter to bring some beer. It is, of course, his product. He slowly pours the contents of the bottle into three glasses.

A number of the films show people at play. One features a group of girls having a pillow fight. Soon the pillows rip apart and the frame is filled with clouds of feathers. Another includes a group of boys playing marbles in the street. A third shows a sack race among Lumière employees. Most of the racers make a few hops and then disappear off camera to the right. It ends with what might be film's first "lovable loser." It is man who stumbles several times and finishes last. He is surrounded by well-wishers—and stumbles again when one claps him on the back.

The Lumières showed that they were already progressing beyond straight documentary with a film called *A Sprinkler Sprinkled*. It was a remake (yet another way in which the Lumière brothers anticipated future film conventions) of their original *A Little Trick on the Gardener*. It also anticipated something that movies do quite often. It adapted material from other sources. In this case, the idea came from a well-known cartoon.

As the film begins, a gardener is watering some of his plants with a hose. A boy creeps up behind him. He steps on the hose, which stops the flow of water. The gardener looks into the end of the hose to see why the water has stopped flowing. The boy takes his foot off the hose. A stream of water pours into the gardener's face. Audiences howled with laughter. It was the beginning of slapstick humor, which would soon become a staple of the film industry. But that isn't the end of the film. The boy tries to run away. He disappears off camera, with the gardener right behind him. A moment later, the gardener drags him by the ear back into the scene. Then he spanks him. The boy rushes off camera. The film ends the same way as it began, with the gardener watering his plants. The boy doesn't get away with his trick.

After *Workers Leaving the Lumière Factory*, probably their most famous film is *The Arrival of a Train at la Ciotat Station*. It begins with an image of a train in the distance. The locomotive rapidly grows larger as it approaches the camera. According to a contemporary newspaper, many of the spectators screamed in fright as they watched the train approach. Some got up and tried to run away. (Other sources say this didn't happen. The audience sat calmly during the entire film.) The locomotive rushes out of the frame to the left. Moments later, it halts. The platform becomes a beehive of activity. Dozens of people get on and off the train.

Some of their films appear to be very simple. Critics dismiss these as nothing more than home movies. One of the most famous of this type is

Feeding the Baby. Auguste and his wife sit at a table with their baby between them. This apparent simplicity is misleading. Louis's extensive background in photography had given him a strong sense of composition. The scene is carefully framed. It reveals that the family is well off, living in a large house with a garden and wearing good clothing. They have the opportunity for relaxing "quality time" with their baby. Only a successful man could enjoy this type of lifestyle.

Other films feature very complex interactions. In one, the camera is set up on one side of a river. Occupying the lower part of the frame on the opposite side is a group of women. They work hard as they wash clothing in the river. At the top of the frame is a roadway. Carriages and pedestrians hurry along in both directions. The center is an area of calm in the midst of the frenzied action at the top and bottom of the frame. Several men stand there. They don't do anything except stare at the camera. Perhaps the cameraman was making a statement about the relative roles of men and women.

These early films withstand the test of time. The action is clear and easy to follow. Louis took several versions of each film. He made slight changes of exposure and composition. He chose the best one to show.

Louis made the first few dozen films, using the firm's one camera. He didn't make more than a few afterward. He soon became a producer. After the success of their Paris exhibition, there was a clamor for the Lumières to sell their Cinématographes. That may have been their original plan. Now the circumstances had changed. They made dozens of the devices, but they had no intention of selling them. Instead, they trained many men as operators. They equipped them with Cinématographes and film, and sent them around the world.

One meaning of *Lumière* is "light." Another is "intelligence." The Lumières knew how to appeal to audiences thousands of miles away. As film historian Kenneth Macgowan comments, "Lumière's hand-cranked machine was light, and, because he knew that most towns had no electricity, he used an ether lamp. When one of his representatives reached a new district, he announced that he would take moving pictures of the place and the people, and add them to the show. This not only advertised the new wonder. When the local pictures flashed on the screen, even the most cynical peasant was convinced that here was no trickery."[1]

When the cameramen returned, the Lumières had plenty of footage for their showings. The cameramen had also created priceless images for the future. These images reveal the details of daily life from a bygone era to viewers today.

Their cameramen also pioneered new techniques. Standard procedure was to set up the Cinématographe in one place and do the filming without moving it. One of the cameramen mounted his Cinématographe on a gondola, a type of boat, while he was shooting scenes in Venice, Italy. It was the first moving shot. When the cameraman returned, he was afraid he'd be yelled at. Instead, Louis was impressed. He ordered his other cameramen to begin adding similar shots.

The best foreign market was the United States. There, more than 20 Lumière cameramen were at work. Félix Mesguich was one of them. He commented, "You had to have lived these moments of collective exaltation, have attended these thrilling screenings in order to understand how far the excitement of the crowd could go. With a flick of the switch, I plunge several thousand spectators into darkness. Each scene passes, accompanied by tempestuous applause; after the sixth scene, I return the hall to light. The audience is shaking. Cries ring out: 'The Lumière Brothers, the Lumière Brothers!' "[2]

Writing at the same time, a *New York Dramatic Mirror* reporter noted: "Lumière's Cinématographes created a decided sensation here last week. . . . The audiences were very enthusiastic over the new discovery. . . . A lecturer was employed to explain the pictures as they were shown, but he was hardly necessary, as the views speak for themselves."[3]

As word spread across the country, the demand for films soared. People enjoyed seeing exotic foreign lands. They also enjoyed seeing familiar scenes from their own hometowns.

The honeymoon ended abruptly. Under President William McKinley, the country had adopted an "America first" attitude. It didn't go over well that "foreigners" were "taking over" an American business, especially one that had been pioneered by the famous and beloved Thomas Edison. The Lumières began to encounter serious discrimination. Advertisements played up the good points of American technology while putting down Lumière equipment. Mesguich was thrown in jail because he was allegedly filming without a proper permit. The Customs Service accused the company of bringing cameras into the country illegally. Some cameramen were threatened with bodily harm. By the summer of 1897, Lumière's men had fled back to the safety of their native country.

By 1898, the Lumières issued a catalog—their seventh—that listed more than 1,400 individual titles. The majority had been shot by their hardworking overseas cameramen. Most were scenic films that showed a particular aspect of the country's landscape. A few were forerunners of modern-day newscasts. One showed scenes of minor flooding near Lyon. Another showed the visit of the Russian czar to France.

Today, we would call such coverage "soft news." The brothers were products of their times. Their films reflect the living conditions of well-off French citizens, in which controversy was kept to a minimum. They had little interest in "hard news." In particular, they made little effort to cover the Dreyfus Affair. It began at about the same time as their invention of the Cinématographe and soon polarized France.

They also had little interest in continuing in the movie business. Their success spawned a host of rivals. Many merely imitated the Lumières' style and subjects. It became increasingly difficult to compete. Their last major contribution came in 1900. They designed a giant screen as part of the Universal Exhibition in Paris and made some films that were shown on the screen. Within a few years, they had returned to their roots. In 1903, they patented Autochrome Lumière, a type of color film for still photography.

There was no shortage of filmmakers to take their place—and they would change the course of the budding film industry.

Captain Alfred Dreyfus

French filmmakers in the United States were not the only ones to face discrimination. In France in 1894, discarded papers were discovered in a wastebasket. These papers made it appear that a French army officer was supplying secret information to the Germans. Suspicion fell on Captain Alfred Dreyfus. The primary "evidence" against him was that he had access to the information—and that he was Jewish. At the time, the French army was decidedly anti-Jewish. Dreyfus was tried and convicted in a court-martial on the basis of flimsy evidence, which he hadn't been allowed to examine. He was publicly humiliated and sentenced to life imprisonment on Devil's Island, a harsh penal colony off the northern coast of South America.

Two years later, the newly appointed army intelligence chief, Lieutenant Colonel Georges Picquart, reexamined the evidence. Though he was anti-Jewish, he believed that Dreyfus was innocent. He also believed that the real traitor, Ferdinand Walsin Esterhazy, was still giving information to the Germans. The French army seemed more concerned with preserving its image than in uncovering the truth. After a brief trial early in 1898, the army banished Picquart to North Africa and acquitted Esterhazy.

At that point, noted French author Émile Zola wrote a newspaper article entitled "J'Accuse!" (I accuse!), accusing the army of a cover-up. In turn, the army charged him of libel. He had to flee to England to avoid being arrested. His article served to divide the country into two factions. On one side were those who favored a monarchy, the military, and the Catholic Church. On the other were liberals, those who favored a republican form of government, and many who wanted to curb the power of the Catholic Church.

Later that year, it became apparent that most of the evidence against Dreyfus had been forged. Even with this revelation, Dreyfus was again found guilty when he was retried by another military court. In 1899, French President Émile Loubet pardoned Dreyfus and allowed him to return to France. His name wasn't cleared until 1906, at which time he was restored to his military rank.

Born in 1861, Georges Méliès is often credited with being the first man to tell stories on screen. When he began his film career in 1896, he used many new techniques. These included special effects. He died in 1938.

4

Telling Stories

Georges Méliès was among the first people to see the Lumières' work when the exhibition opened in Paris. To him, it seemed little short of miraculous. He approached Auguste Lumière, offering to pay any amount of money to be able to use the Cinématographe.

"Lumière would not listen to me," he recalled. " 'Young man,' said he, 'you should be grateful, since although my invention is not for sale, it would undoubtedly ruin you. It can be exploited for a certain time as a scientific curiosity, but, apart from that, it has no commercial future whatsoever.' "[1]

In view of the profound influence that movies have today, Auguste's statement seems like one of the worst predictions ever made. Yet there was a kernel of truth in his observation. Had films continued to be exclusively documentary in nature, they might have quickly fallen out of favor.

As British filmmaker Robert W. Paul said in 1898, "The public has seen too many trains, trams and autobuses. And with the exception of a few films . . . one could say that no one up to now has begun to exploit the possibilities of moving pictures, to make us laugh, cry, or be amazed."[2]

In other words, audiences wanted to see stories. Méliès was about to satisfy that desire. He came from a very different environment than the Lumières. He was a theater manager who had a wide variety of job experiences under his belt. He shrugged off the Lumières' rejection, bought a similar camera, and adapted it for his own purposes. One of his first films showed how different he was from the Lumières. Made in 1896, it was *The Devil's Castle,* a three-minute film that is probably history's first horror movie. In 1899, he made the first film with more than a single scene. That same year he also made *Dreyfus Affair,* a 15-minute dramatized version of the controversial events dividing France. The film caused an uproar and was soon banned. Three years later he produced *A Trip to the Moon.* It was based on Jules Verne's novel *From the Earth to the Moon.* It had 30 separate scenes, lasted for about 20 minutes, and became his most famous and profitable film.

Méliès soon lost some of his influence. People grew tired of his fantasies and his often outlandish special effects. They wanted more realistic stories. Other French filmmakers such as Léon Gaumont and the brothers Charles and Émile Pathé fulfilled this demand. They surpassed Méliès in importance.

France wasn't the only country making films. Italy was also important. Germany, Russia, England, Scandinavia, and other European countries were beginning to develop their own movie industries.

Across the Atlantic Ocean, the United States was about to regain the momentum that it had originally had with Edison's inventions. Edison himself hadn't been inactive. He developed his own projector. In 1896, he produced *The Kiss.* It showed two famous Broadway actors kissing. It provoked outrage from many people. They believed it was "immoral" to see people smooching on the big screen. Among other innovations, he developed a camera small enough to be taken outdoors.

Dozens of film companies sprang up in the United States. Because the industry was so new, there were hardly any laws or regulations governing it. These companies routinely ignored patents and pirated films from one another.

This chaos was too much for Edison, who was a ruthless businessman. Starting in 1898, he began bringing lawsuits against any company that he believed used any of his patents without his permission. At first he went after smaller companies. Then he took on the large ones.

An Edison employee named Edwin S. Porter made the first big American hit film, *The Great Train Robbery*, in 1903. Consisting of 14 scenes, it featured numerous innovative camera techniques. These included one of the first close-ups in film history. At the end of the film, one of the bandits aims his gun directly at the audience. It probably made some people jump out of their seats. The film earned a great deal of money for Edison and helped to fuel the public's desire for story films.

Thomas Edison's first projector was the Vitascope. It was introduced in 1896. It was replaced later that year with the Edison Projecting Kinetoscope.

Two years later, a Pittsburgh businessman named Harry Davis rented a store. He installed dozens of seats and showed 20-minute films with piano accompaniment from midmorning to midnight. He charged a nickel for admission. That price was well within the reach of most people. His theater became known as a nickelodeon. Within a few years there were more than 8,000 nickelodeons in the country. They attracted millions of viewers and created a tremendous demand for new films.

To control this lucrative market, Edison changed his strategy. He dropped his lawsuits against the large competitors and formed the Motion Picture Patents Company. It consisted of the nine largest studios (Edison's and others such as Vitagraph and Biograph); the country's leading film distributor; and Eastman Kodak, which agreed to sell film only to the Patents Company. In theory, the agreement would allow only company members to produce and distribute films in the United States.

They were quickly opposed by a number of independent producers, who used either pirated equipment or equipment imported from Europe. The Patents Company fought back—figuratively and literally. They hired lawyers and took the independents to court. They also hired private investigators. Many were little more than goons. Sometimes the investigators broke into the independent producers' studios. They smashed cameras and beat up whomever they found there.

Despite their differences, however, the Patents Company and the independents had one thing in common. Their actors were anonymous. In some cases, the actors themselves wanted to keep their names secret. "Serious" actors—those who had successful stage careers— didn't want to be identified with films. They considered movie work to be much less prestigious than live theater. Of more influence was the attitude of the film companies. They were afraid that if the actors were identified, they would become famous and demand more money.

Slowly the Patents Company gained the upper hand in the struggle with independents. The independents found several ways to fight back. One was to create the star system. Another was taking the Patents Company to court on the grounds that it was an illegal monopoly. Third was the reversal of an old adage that goes, "If you can't beat 'em, join 'em." To the independents, joining the Patents Company was not an option. They did the opposite. They ran away—as far as they could. Their destination was a sleepy valley in Southern California that hardly anyone back East had ever heard of.

It was Hollywood.

Florence Lawrence

The first famous screen actor was Florence Lawrence. Born in Canada in 1886 to a vaudeville performer, Florence became involved in show business at the age of four. She made her film debut in 1907 with Vitagraph. The following year, D. W. Griffith lured her to Biograph by offering more money.

She was busy at Biograph, making 38 movies in 1908 and 65 in 1909. People began to notice her. Many wrote to Biograph asking for her name. Biograph refused to release it. The company simply referred to her as the Biograph Girl.

In 1910, Carl Laemmle formed the Independent Motion Picture Company. He wanted to give his new company a boost in his struggle against the Patents Company. He offered Lawrence much more money than she had received at Biograph. Then he started a rumor that the "Biograph Girl" had died in an accident. Not long afterward, he bought huge newspaper ads. The ads revealed that she was alive and would begin appearing in IMP films. He arranged for a personal appearance in St. Louis. She attracted more people than President William Howard Taft, who had visited the city a week before.

Her name appeared on theater marquees next to film titles. Within a few years, she was earning a lot of money. She bought an expensive car. Proving that she had both beauty and brains, she invented the first turn and brake signals.

In 1915, she was seriously injured in a studio fire. By the time she recovered, the film-going public had found other actors to idolize. She tried to make a comeback but could never get much more than bit parts.

Her personal life turned tragic. Her first two husbands died. Her third marriage lasted only a year. The Great Depression wiped her out financially. Suffering from a painful disease, she committed suicide in 1938. She was buried in an unmarked grave. In 1991, actor Roddy McDowall paid for a headstone to mark the site. It identifies her as "The First Movie Star."

This photo of the Lumière brothers was taken late in their lives. By then they had received many honors for their pioneering work in motion pictures. They were also responsible for innovative achievements in color still photography.

5

Heading West

For the independents, Hollywood had several benefits. Perhaps the most obvious was the climate. The sun was still the only source of reliable light. In California it shone nearly year-round. Movies were becoming more and more complex. It was important to be able to plan a shooting schedule and keep to it. It was much more difficult to do that in the East, where the weather was uncertain.

California boasted a wide variety of scenery. Within an hour or two of Hollywood, film producers could find almost anything they needed: ocean beaches, mountains, forests, deserts, lakes, large towns and small villages, and more.

Land in Southern California was cheap. So was labor. Taxes were low.

There was one other practical advantage. If the hired thugs from the Patents Company threatened to show up, it was a simple matter to load everything into a few cars and flee across the border to Mexico until things cooled down.

In Hollywood, the independents took advantage of the new popularity of feature-length films. These were films that lasted for at least one hour. Some studios made several of these films every week.

They had an eagerly awaiting audience. By that time there were thousands of movie theaters in the country.

It also helped that Europe was in the grip of World War I. Celluloid was the main ingredient in movie film. It contained the same chemicals that were used in explosives. European governments decided that killing enemies was more important than entertainment. There was very little film available on the continent. The lack of film almost eliminated the competition from European filmmakers, especially those in France and Italy. In addition, it opened new markets for American films. They became one of the most eagerly anticipated imports in Europe as the war raged on. According to some estimates, the United States accounted for about half of all films made in 1914. Four years later, nearly all were American.

By then, the independents had gained the upper hand. In 1915, the Patents Company was declared to be an illegal monopoly. Two years later, it was disbanded. Nearly all of its members had already gone out of business. The rest would soon follow. Hollywood had become the movie capital of the United States. Its influence extended around the globe. A decade earlier, the independents had struggled to survive. Now they became major studios such as Paramount, Universal, 20th Century Fox, and Warner Brothers. They all featured big stars whose presence in a film almost always guaranteed box-office success.

Like the companies that had been part of the Patents Company, the silent-film era was about to disappear as well. Sound films would transform the movie landscape.

In addition to their other contributions to filmmaking, the Lumières had pioneered a primitive form of movie sound. During the screening of the conversation between Janssen and Lagrange at the Congress of the French Photographic Society, the two men stood behind the screen. They had the same conversation that had been filmed. They tried to repeat it exactly. That way the words coming from behind the screen would match what the audience was seeing.

More realistically, filmmakers starting with Edison had tried to add synchronized sound. Right away they encountered two problems. One was amplifying sound to fill the large space of a theater. The other was synchronizing two machines. One played the film and one played the sound. It was virtually impossible to get them to operate together.

Both problems were solved in the mid-1920s. Improved sound equipment allowed everyone in even the largest theaters to hear what was being said. It also became possible to put the sound track onto the film itself. Filmmakers didn't need two different machines anymore. The sound and the picture played at the same time.

In 1927, the first successful sound film, *The Jazz Singer,* was released. The movie and its immediate successors proved to be so popular that studios adopted sound as standard on films. After the basic invention of motion pictures, adding sound was the biggest single advance in movie technology. To obtain the best possible sound quality, the silent-film standard of 16 frames per second was increased to the current 24 frames per second.

Just as "moving pictures" became "movies," the new "talking pictures" became known as "talkies." The advent of talkies had an unexpected consequence. Some silent-film stars had high-pitched, squeaky voices that were unsuited for sound. Audiences laughed at

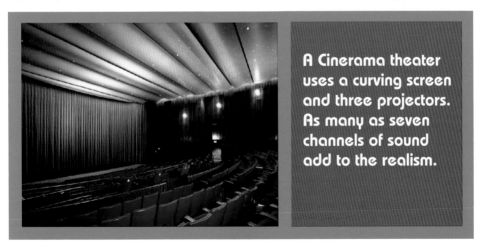

A Cinerama theater uses a curving screen and three projectors. As many as seven channels of sound add to the realism.

One of the most famous films in movie history is *The Jazz Singer*. It was the first "talkie," a movie with synchronized sound. Its star, Al Jolson, appears to be an African American. In reality he was a Caucasian who used makeup to darken his face.

them. Their careers were over. Others had such strong accents that audiences could barely understand them. They too were finished.

The following decade saw the first widespread use of color film. Since then, many other advances have made the movie-going experience even more meaningful. Projection techniques such as Cinerama made audiences feel more involved in the on-screen action. Special effects became increasingly realistic. Movie stars commanded ever-larger salaries as it became obvious that they were vitally important to the success of the films in which they appeared. Because of these factors and others, millions of people go to movie theaters every year. Many more enjoy watching movies at home on video and DVD players.

The brothers survived long enough to see many of these changes. Louis lived until June 6, 1948. Auguste died on April 10, 1954. Their company lasted even longer. In 1982, it was purchased by Ilford, one of the world's largest film manufacturers. It became known as Ilford France.

It wasn't the end of the Lumière name. That same year—1982—the family mansion became the Lumière Institute. The institute is a center for film study and research. In 1995, an estimated 400,000 people poured into Lyon for a series of events commemorating the 100th anniversary of the original screening. Three years later, a state-of-the-art movie theater called the Lumière Theater was erected on the site of the original factory.

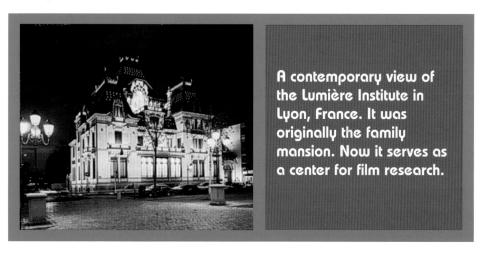

A contemporary view of the Lumière Institute in Lyon, France. It was originally the family mansion. Now it serves as a center for film research.

If the Lumière brothers were alive today and making films, their movies would probably be good enough to be shown at that theater—and in many other theaters around the world.

1953 Academy Award

Founded in Hollywood in May 1927, the Academy of Motion Picture Arts and Sciences originally had 36 members. They were production executives and other prominent figures associated with the film industry. Today the Academy boasts more than 6,000 members. It is best known for its annual presentation of the Academy Awards, nicknamed Oscars because of the statues given to the winners in each category. The most common explanation for the nickname is that an Academy employee commented that the statue resembled her uncle Oscar.

The first Academy Awards were presented at a banquet in May 1929. Films released between August 1927 and July 1928 were eligible. There was none of the suspense associated with today's Academy Awards. The winners had been announced three months earlier. The awards were virtually identical to the ones given out today: a figure standing on top of a roll of film. German actor Emil Jannings had to return home before the ceremony. He became the first person to receive an Oscar, because the Academy presented it to him before he left. The World War I drama Wings received the first Oscar for Best Picture.

The following year, part of the ceremony was broadcast over the radio. Ever since then, the Academy Awards have been broadcast either on the radio or on television. Starting with the fourth Academy Awards, the names of the winners were kept secret until the night of the ceremony to add suspense. One of the most memorable episodes happened two years later. Comedian Will Rogers, the master of ceremonies, announced that the winner of the Oscar for Best Director was "my good friend Frank." Both Frank Capra and Frank Lloyd began walking forward. After an embarrassed moment, Rogers clarified the situation. Lloyd was the winner.

Today, the Academy Awards show is one of the most-watched television events in the world. According to estimates, more than a billion viewers all over the world tune in. The buildup begins months before the ceremony. Getting nominated for an Oscar almost always brings additional box-office revenue.

Chronology

1862 August Lumière is born.

1864 Louis Lumière is born.

1895 Lumière brothers patent the Cinématographe; they exhibit 10 films in the first commercial screening for an audience.

1896 Lumière cameramen begin filming around the world.

1900 Lumières build giant Cinématographe screen at Universal Exhibition in Paris.

1903 The Lumières patent Autochrome Lumière, color film for still photography.

1911 Antoine Lumière dies.

1939 The Cannes Film Festival is scheduled to open, with Louis Lumière as honorary chairman; the outbreak of World War II cancels it.

1948 Louis Lumière dies.

1954 Auguste Lumière dies.

1982 The Lumière family mansion becomes the site of the Lumière Institute, a film and research facility.

1995 An estimated 400,000 visitors come to Lyon for ceremonies marking the 100th anniversary of the first commercial film screening.

1998 A state-of-the-art movie theater is built on the site of Lumière factory, the scene of Louis Lumière's first film.

Timeline of Discovery

1826	Joseph Nicéphore Niepce produces the world's first photographic image.
1837	Louis Daguerre invents the daguerreotype, the first practical method of portrait photography.
1877	Thomas Edison invents the phonograph. Eadweard Muybridge takes action pictures of racehorses.
1889	George Eastman invents celluloid roll film.
1891	Thomas Edison employee William Dickson develops the prototype of the Kinetoscope.
1893	Dickson constructs a revolving workshop known as Black Maria to produce Kinetoscope films.
1894	In the Dreyfus Affair, Alfred Dreyfus is wrongly convicted of selling French army secrets to Germany.
1895	German scientist Wilhelm Roentgen discovers X-rays.
1902	Georges Méliès produces *A Trip to the Moon*.
1908	The Motion Picture Patents Company is established to control the production of movies and their distribution in the United States.
1910	Florence Lawrence becomes the first movie star.
1927	Philo T. Farnsworth sends the first television picture using electricity. Academy of Motion Pictures Arts and Sciences is founded. *The Jazz Singer* becomes the first successful "talkie."
1929	The stock market crash plunges the United States into the Great Depression. The first Academy Awards are presented; *Wings* is named Best Picture.
1937	Walt Disney's *Snow White and the Seven Dwarfs* becomes the first full-length color animated film.
1946	The Cannes Film Festival is held for the first time; director Frank Capra makes *It's a Wonderful Life*, the showing of which becomes an annual Christmas season tradition.
1952	The Cinerama process makes its debut, using three projectors on a wide, curving screen.
1964	*A Fistful of Dollars* is Clint Eastwood's first major movie role.
1975	Director Steven Spielberg releases *Jaws*, which becomes the highest-grossing film to that point.
1977	*Star Wars*, the first of George Lucas's nine-part science fiction series, is released.
2004	*The Return of the King* sets a record by winning all 11 Academy Awards for which it is nominated; it ties *Ben-Hur* (1959) and *Titanic* (1997) for most total Oscars.
2005	Comedian Chris Rock hosts the 77th Academy Awards before a worldwide television audience of more than one billion; director Clint Eastwood's *Million Dollar Baby* wins the Oscar for Best Picture.

Chapter Notes

Chapter Two: The Cinématographe

    1. Alan Williams, *Republic of Images: A History of French Filmmaking* (Cambridge, MA: Harvard University Press, 1992), p. 22.

    2. Chris Dashiell, "The Oldest Movies," http://www.cinescene.com/dash/lumiere.html.

Chapter Three: Filming Around the World

    1. Kenneth Macgowan, *Behind the Screen: The History and Techniques of the Motion Picture* (New York: Delacorte Press, 1965), p. 92.

    2. Emmanuelle Toulet, *Birth of the Motion Picture*, translated by Susan Emanuel (New York: Henry N. Abrams, Inc., 1998), pp. 20–21.

    3. Frank E. Beaver, *On Film: A History of the Motion Picture* (New York: McGraw Hill Book Company, 1983), p. 3.

Chapter Four: Telling Stories

    1. Maurice Bardeche and Robert Brasillach, *The History of Motion Pictures*, translated and edited by Iris Barry (New York: Arno Press, 1970), p. 10.

    2. Emmanuelle Toulet, *Birth of the Motion Picture*, translated by Susan Emanuel (New York: Henry N. Abrams, Inc., 1998), p. 111.

Further Reading

For Young Adults

Adair, Gene. *Thomas Alva Edison: Inventing the Electric Age*. New York: Oxford University Press, 1996.

Cross, Robin. *Movie Magic*. New York: Sterling Publishing Co., 1995.

Hamilton, Jake. *Special Effects in Film and Television*. New York: DK Publishing, 1998.

Murcia, Rebecca Thatcher. *Thomas Edison: Great Inventor*. Hockessin, DE: Mitchell Lane Publishers, 2004.

O'Brien, Lisa. *Lights, Camera, Action: Making Movies and TV from the Inside Out*. Toronto, Canada: Owl Books, 1998.

Platt, Richard. *Film*. New York: Alfred A. Knopf, 1992.

Works Consulted

Abel, Richard. *The Ciné Goes to Town: French Cinema, 1896–1914*. Berkeley, CA: University of California Press, 1994.

Armes, Roy. *French Cinema*. London: Secker & Warburg, 1985.

Bardeche, Maurice, and Robert Brasillach. *The History of Motion Pictures*. Translated and edited by Iris Barry. New York: Arno Press, 1970.

Beaver, Frank E. *On Film: A History of the Motion Picture*. New York: McGraw Hill Book Company, 1983.

Fell, John L., editor. *Film Before Griffith*. Berkeley, CA: University of California Press, 1983.

Lanzoni, Remi Fournier. *French Cinema: From Its Beginnings to the Present*. New York: Continuum, 2002.

Macgowan, Kenneth. *Behind the Screen: The History and Techniques of the Motion Picture*. New York: Delacorte Press, 1965.

Shipman, David. *The Story of Cinema*. New York: St. Martin's Press, 1982.

Sklar, Robert. *Film: An International History of the Medium*. New York: Harry N. Abrams, 1993.

Toulet, Emmanuelle. *Birth of the Motion Picture*. Translated by Susan Emanuel. New York: Henry N. Abrams, Inc., 1998.

Williams, Alan. *Republic of Images: A History of French Filmmaking*. Cambridge, MA: Harvard University Press, 1992.

On the Internet

Academy of Motion Picture Arts and Sciences: "History and Structure of the Academy of Motion Picture Arts and Sciences"
http://www.oscars.org/academy/history.html

"The Affair"—The Case of Alfred Dreyfus
http://www.wfu.edu/~sinclair/dreyfus.htm

Beals, Gerald. *Biography of Thomas Alva Edison.*
http://www.thomasedison.com/biog.htm

Dashiell, Chris. "The Oldest Movies."
http://www.cinescene.com/dash/lumiere.html

Early Cinema.com: "An Introduction to Early Cinema"
http://www.earlycinema.com/index.html

"Florence Lawrence"
http://www.ftppro.com/library/Florence_Lawrence

"The History of the Academy Awards"
http://history1900s.about.com/library/weekly/aa030801a.htm

Internet Movie Database: "Academy Awards, USA"
http://www.imdb.com/Sections/Awards/Academy_Awards_USA/

Lumière Institute (Home Page)
http://www.institut-lumiere.org/english/frames.html

"Lumière Institute"
http://www.lyon.fr/vdl/sections/en/culture/musees/institut_lumiere/

Northern Stars: "Florence Lawrence"
http://www.northernstars.ca/actorsjkl/lawrencebio.html

Scott, E. Kilburn. "Adventures in CyberSound: The Career of L.A.A. Le Prince"
http://www.acmi.net.au/AIC/LE_PRINCE_JSMPTE.html

Glossary

celluloid (SELL-yuh-loid)—transparent material derived from cellulose, the cell walls of plants; it is the main ingredient in photographic film.

conventions (kuhn-VENT-shuns)—customary or generally agreed-on ways of doing things.

Customs Service (KUSS-tums SIR-vuss)—the federal agency that regulates imports and exports.

cynical (SIH-nih-kuhl)—distrustful of human nature.

dictaphone (DIK-tuh-fone)—a device used to record a person talking.

discrimination (dis-krih-muh-NAY-shun)—acting against a certain group or individual.

exposure time (ik-SPOE-zhur TIME)—the length of time a camera shutter remains open, allowing light to pass through the lens and reach the film.

insomnia (in-SAHM-nee-uh)—the inability to fall asleep or remain asleep.

intermittent (in-ter-MIH-tunt)—not continuous; starting and stopping at intervals.

libel (LIE-bull)—writing that conveys a false and damaging impression of a person or group.

lucrative (LOO-kruh-tiv)—very profitable.

mimeograph (MIH-mee-oh-graf)—a device used to make copies of a document by forcing ink through a stencil.

monopoly (muh-NAH-puh-lee)—having complete control of an industry; not allowing competitors.

patent (PAA-tunt)—the legal recognition of the right of an inventor for sole use of the invention for a certain period of time.

polarize (POE-luh-rize)—to divide into two opposing sides.

shutter (SHUH-tur)—the cover that opens over a tiny hole to admit a certain amount of light into a camera, then closes to keep further light from entering.

slapstick (SLAP-stik)—a type of humor that relies on physical comedy rather than spoken jokes.

synchronized (SING-kruh-nized)—happening or operating at the same time or in sequence together.

take the uninterrupted filming of a scene.

tempestuous (tem-PESS-choo-us)—stormy, turbulent.

Index